# Letter to Auden

# Letter to Auden
N.S. Thompson

Published 2010 by
Smokestack Books
PO Box 408, Middlesbrough TS5 6WA
e-mail : info@smokestack-books.co.uk
www.smokestack-books.co.uk

**Letter to Auden**
N.S. Thompson
Cover image: Simon Fieldhouse
Author photo: Gerry Cambridge

Printed by
EPW Print & Design Ltd

ISBN 978-0-9564175-1-0
Smokestack Books gratefully
acknowledges the support of
Arts Council England

Smokestack Books is
represented by Inpress Ltd
www.inpressbooks.co.uk

'Greed showing shamelessly her naked money,
And all Love's wondering eloquence debased
To a collector's slang, Smartness in furs,
And Beauty scratching miserably for food,
Honour self-sacrificed for Calculation,
And Reason stoned by Mediocrity,
Freedom by Power shockingly maltreated,
And Justice exiled till Saint Geoffrey's Day.

So in this hour of crisis and dismay
What better than your strict and adult pen
Can warn us from the colours and the consolations,
The showy arid works, reveal
The squalid shadow of academy and garden,
Make action urgent and its nature clear?
Who give us nearer insight to resist
The expanding fear, the savaging disaster?'

W H Auden, 'To Christopher Isherwood'

# PART I

'Dear Wystan' is the way I should begin
This letter to you, but today I fear
It may seem offhand or ungenuine:
'Dear Auden' is archaic, even 'dear'
These days is taken to be too sincere,
Unless you mean it. No wish to offend,
So could you take the first as from a friend?

Not that we ever met, although we crossed
Paths once in Ilkley by the famous moor
The year you passed away and, yes, I tossed
Away the opportunity, too poor
To cough up for your reading. Such a bore,
But then a local adage urging 'sup all'
Convinced me for a pub-crawl with Jeff Nuttall.

Please, Wystan, overlook this sin of youth.
I know it's inexcusable to miss
A maestro's reading and I was uncouth
(An ignorance that sadly brought no bliss),
Though happily a metamorphosis
Occurred and if I am still drinking hard
It is no longer with the avant-garde...

Oh, dear, I notice something else amiss
    Besides the lack of deference in address;
It seems that if you write verse such as this
    Tradition says it wears a formal dress;
    A glance at the above and I confess
To overlooking that it should indent.
Forgive me, Wystan, no offence was meant.

Like you, I thought to use *ottava rima*
    In homage to the noble Gordon, George –
Lord Byron – but the extra line could seem a...
    Well, should we say too mighty to disgorge
    Mere gossip? So, if from a lesser forge,
I hope there is some mettle in the blend.
And any faulty numbers, please amend...

Up to a point, that is. You liked to tinker
    With everything you wrote, even omitted
Works from the canon. Mark of a great thinker?
    I think not. And it has to be admitted
    Rarely improved on what you first committed
To print.  But we can read the job well done
Imprimis, thanks to Edward Mendelson.

Now let's begin the fun here, rock and roll,
    Break open several bottles and get sloshed,
And if my measures do lack some control,
    Then who would notice? Thus my hands are washed.
    But in this letter to you, nothing's quashed,
It comes with all the news that's fit to hear.
There's mountains of it. Got your mountain gear?

I doubt you need to call for oxygen,
    Although there's plenty that will make you gasp;
It could be some detachment such as Zen
    Would help, but then you liked to get a grasp
    Of things and were a sponge; the facts may rasp
At times, but there is nothing hard to swallow...
At least it's not an Oracle of Apollo.

And I would never claim to be prophetic.
    A poet's disappointing if, like Blake,
He's tempted to be broadly theoretic
    And lays a grand design out for our sake.
    So I will humbly dig about and rake
Up what you need for keeping up to speed...
And, after all, you have some time to read.

You gathered every kind of information,
    Reviewing many different types of books
From scientific texts to education,
    And surely it was not a writer's looks
    Attracted you; yes, you could get your hooks
In population growth and cereal,
The metabolic or bacterial,

And with a journalistic touch for issues
    Turned molehills into mountains; and, on love,
Were softer than a pile of well-used tissues
    (Things any better now with those above?)
    But seemed to have a hand in every glove
And, as you learned from Bert Brecht and Kurt Weill,
Mixed poetry and politics with style.

If I can hardly hope to emulate
    You there, I see there is a kind of fun
In being flippant as you flagellate;
    But still, it must be said, I feel the gun
    At my head too and want to make a run
For it: but then it's ringing like a bell
This is a year that homages will sell.

Oh, yes, your anniversary's been news
    (Up to a point): pundits and critics tried
To formulate you in as many views
    As have accumulated since you died.
    I hope you will forgive them if they lied,
There is delight in hagiography
Despite the blots in your biography.

That's not to say there will not be a shelf
    Of books about you this year and besides,
What poet wants to read about himself?
    You flickered in and out of many tides
    Of thought and fashion, mainly for the rides
They offered, all exciting in your day.
Perhaps you slightly envied Hemingway?

I will refrain myself on all accounts
    (Well, for a little while at least): you were
A paradox and anyone who mounts
    The podium to explicate the blur
    Of whirling images may cause a stir,
But thankfully that here is not my task.
A little time from you is all I ask.

So first, you want the good news or the bad?
  There's global warming, climate havoc, war
From Dafur to the suburbs of Baghdad
  And not a great deal to be hopeful for…
  Before we go through that particular door
Perhaps we should kick off with a surprise
For you: our world's gone mad for enterprise.

Yes, with the Eastern Bloc as driving force
  In '89 came Communism's end,
(The Soviets reluctantly, of course)
  But Velvet Revolutions set the trend
  And party leaders reaped the dividend.
Perhaps the Russian mafia puts on airs,
But then why not? They're multibillionaires!

The Federation has its sister states,
  Each hoping for an upturn from decline,
A president who seldom delegates,
  Would never put dissenters down a mine,
  But manages to make them all incline
In his direction, calling 'democratic'
What unambiguously is autocratic.

With aging Soviet missiles all kaput,
  The Cold War safe as history, now there's oil
To field as economic weapon, shut
  Supply off to a client less than loyal,
  And make a better deal on foreign soil:
With power in the pipeline, there are those
Who have a godlike power to dispose.

Out in the Far East, it's a different story.
  The year you died, I think saw Vietnam
Fall. For America there was no glory,
  But then Red China courted Uncle Sam
  And in a decade with designs, a dam
Or two, its output grew and now supplies
Computers, sportswear, toys and print silk ties.

The Yellow River's under yellow smog,
    Its factories a throwback to the scene
Your childhood Midlands had and now they hog
    The markets, too. The Dragon may be green
    With dollars, but there's little landscape seen:
In Northern Provinces, it's touch and go
Where coal dust carpets Shanxi's Gerzhuotou.

You knew exactly why the Japanese
    Invaded her in 1938.
They felt the World had brought them to their knees
    When they tried to industrialise the state.
    It will not work unless you motivate
Production by the market and the test
Was how much it could win back from the West.

Oh yes, I find it quite familiar
    Reading of that dishonest low decade
When nation vied with nation.  Not dissimilar?
    As yet, we chat; the military parade
    About, while we pump billions in for aid
And oil out and hope to settle scores,
Except in Afghan and Iraqi wars.

At one time it was said a New World Order
    Was taking shape; that would be hard to tell
Now conflict's not confined to any border
    But organized discretely cell by cell:
    Collectively what all the movements spell
Out in the hands that push the envelope
Is simply men and women without hope.

I often wonder who it is prolongs
    The ghetto life? With oil revenues
The Middle East can surely right the wrongs
    There, bring development and start to lose
    The poverty, unless they wish to use
The capital for politics and make
More capital with martyrs at the stake.

No doubt recruiting martyrs for a cause
　　Is difficult, but what is more than sad,
Beyond the tragic death toll, is applause
　　For young lives lost (the lives they never had):
　　It seems the easy option is to add
More to their number, more lives up in smoke,
Told it's the only means against the yoke.

But what's the yoke? If desperation breeds
　　The forces that will actuate revolt,
It's still the higher minds that plant the seeds.
　　The trick is never let the people bolt
　　And have them feel continually the jolt
Of how a Western dominance consumes
The daily profits as its market booms.

Yes, you can find an idealistic young
　　And bombers coming from the middle class,
But you will see it is the ghettos sprung
　　Most into action: if you keep the mass
　　Of people desperate, then the desperate pass
To action. As you said, schoolchildren learn
That evil done breeds evil in return.

I write this from a bed-sit in the sticks
　　Today and yes, like yours, it's warm and snug
But make this survey of world politics
　　While feeling like a bug squashed in a rug
　　On every side of which there is a tug
Of war. My intro starts on this, you see,
News of a New Age of Anxiety.

If there's anxiety, it's caused by change,
　　Acceleration East and West is fast,
Increased mobility means we exchange
　　The goods and services that used to last
　　More rapidly, but change comes with a blast,
Less job security, less loyalty,
But bigger bonus, twice the royalty.

Where ideology is at an end,
     And thoughts are nothing new, but only clones
Of pluralistic freedom, now the trend
     Is working all your waking hours like drones
     Not for the State this time, but for the loans
To bolster national productivity,
Be it the GN or the GDP.

And yet we move about the world in droves
     From economic migrants, refugees,
Backpackers on a gap year from the groves
     Of Academe to businessmen who please
     Themselves where they will set up overseas.
The world we live in is transposable
And, like its products, all disposable.

Time for a break? No, time for taking stock…
     You know, all the above is taking place
From LA to Sri Lanka and Bangkok.
     Society bears an international face:
     Where foods airfreighted more than people race
About the globe, the more jet engines whine
To stock our shelves with strawberries and wine.

Container ships give them ample support,
     It takes no more than sixteen days from Far
East factory to Californian port,
     And distribution then is on a par,
     So what the swingers in a Detroit bar
Are wearing one night could have been in store
Less than a month before in Singapore.

So there you have it, that's about the size
     Of it: if huge economies of scale
Bring any benefit, let's eulogize
     Them, can't help feeling though, that like the whale,
     They're an endangered species bound to fail,
Unless we find new energy to burn
Back to the small and local we return…

The only valid style alternative
    Is putting some contraption on your roof
And growing all the food you need to live
    Means hoping that the greens are insect proof;
    In that way we can all remain aloof,
Our carbon footprints wonderfully small,
When shopping out for trainers in the mall.

But then we phone around the globe for hours,
    And text or e-mail on the Internet,
Possessing new communicative powers
    Inside a jumped up television set
    The like of which you never ever met,
Which means you see us virtually curled
Up surfing in a private website world.

Yes, each with his or her LCD screen
    And individual portion of a curry
Prefers an international cuisine
    With website, blog or channel, and no worry
    That life from Aberdeenshire down to Surrey
Looks all the same – meal in a box to watch
A box, wine by the box – and all top notch.

We live united by the Internet,
    The information superhighway brought
To us with every kind of knowledge set
    In cyberspace, where all things can be bought
    And sold, traded or shared, or virus caught
Downloading from a dodgy site that lured,
But one that fortunately can be cured.

And you, as modern as a breakfast bar,
    Informed as any policeman on the beat,
Authoritative as a culture czar,
    Believed in knowledge if you were to meet
    All poetry's demands and take a seat
On Mount Parnassus. But your *OED*
Has now been superseded by IT.

It's true you had the whole shelf full of twelve
    (Plus any Supplements you could recruit)
And in those orange volumes you would delve
    For prickly or exotic verbal fruit
    With which to grace your lines or what would suit,
For your intention was to inculcate
As much as any wish to dominate...

And dominate you did, a *dominus*
    In prep school, university and page,
And swaggered, a most learned *hominus*,
    Who seemed to know the great men of his age
    (And several women, too), which helped you wage
The dialectic you had with your time,
Sometimes as jester, sometimes pantomime –

But let me get back to the point, and please
    Forgive me, as distracted as I am
(Apologies for these parentheses
    As well, you see, I'm desperate to cram
    The detail in and like *Omar Khayyam*
Force any argument to jump and skip
About a bit) by want of craftsmanship.

But then, you see, today it's still the view,
    Dear Wystan (should you ever wish to know),
The form this letter's in is one that few
    Adopt today and fewer undergo
    As basic training: thus we strike a blow
At centuries of literary oppression,
Élitism and Classical repression...

You sympathise? I know it would be neater
    And certainly have taken far less ink
If I had written this in ballad metre,
    But that would take us to the very brink...
    It has already, now I need a drink.
I'll put down pencil and pick up *The Times*...
I find it very soothing after rhymes.

I also need to bone up on the doom
    And gloom a little more, then take a rest,
Allowing that a lighter mood has room
    As well, but as I put it to the test
    You may not think there's very much to jest
About. It would be hard to call it lyric
And, certainly, it is no panegyric.

# PART II

Your correspondent took a little break
    To read the paper, catch up on the news,
Have it explained more clearly what's at stake:
    A time bomb, namely, and we hold the fuse.
    To switch or not to switch? We have to choose
Between a present and a future course
That leaves, we hope, no feelings of remorse.

This may sound very grand. That's how we talk
    Today, aggrandized like the poet's voice
(But here backed by statistics). Should we balk
    At action? One there for the public choice
    Boys. Can we be unselfish and rejoice
The world could move together? And the poet?
Poets make nothing happen. And they know it.

Like you, I'm going nowhere, here I sit
    And look out at a snowdrift in the garden,
A tiny palm tree's magnified a bit,
    In fact it's one great snowball set to harden...
    I wish this were a trek! So Wystan, pardon
The fact the background here is nothing stoic;
I look out at the ice and that's heroic.

Remember in the 1970s
    There was a clear view of 'the future'?  We
Could live (you said) 'in nylon cubes' or whiz
    About in science-fiction gadgetry,
    Wear what looked like tin foil costumery
While fed from tubes and breeding in them, too.
A vision, fortunately, that's dropped from view...

And with it Aldous Huxley, H. G. Wells,
    George Orwell and Ray Bradbury... All wrote
A public vision of their private hells,
    Hoping this would inspire the antidote
    To inhumanity. What's at our throat
Is equally dramatic, as you heard,
But now let's take a look at the absurd.

I said totalitarian regimes
    Were now restricted to the smaller powers:
In fact we see them every night in schemes
    For our amusement in the smaller hours,
    When strangely we turn into cauliflowers
And sit to oggle people on the box
Who loudly shout and swear and wear no socks.

*Big Brother*'s now reality TV
    And though it has eliminated sex,
It's not via science and technology
    (Nor in reality), but so to vex
    Those simple viewers blessed with rubbernecks
Who hope there's something fruity they can glimpse…
But would TV producers act as pimps?

Self-censorship means they cannot be tempted…
    And, frankly, if that is the sort of thing
From which you would not wish to be exempted,
    Then Continental versions take G-string
    And all the wrapping off. You want to fling
Your eyes in that direction for delight?
You only need connect via satellite.

That only means another metal box,
    Wystan, no need to go to outer space.
This gadget plays the role of rowing cox,
    Giving directions as the signals race
    To earth and, goodness, you should see the pace!
Hundreds of channels at our disposition,
But only one brain each to watch and listen.

Despite the fact that Fahrenheit 451's
    Been superseded to a higher degree
By 9/11 and a million tons
    Collapsing into human tragedy,
    It's good this quasi-documentary
Reminds us of more dangers we could face
And why this New Millennium needs grace.

And if Ray Bradbury saw the end of books
　　When gazing in his futuristic ball,
Envisaging them hauled away in trucks
　　By earnest firemen who took them all
　　As seriously subversive, if you trawl
Among our Big-Bro homes, the lack of shelves
Will tell you we have done the job ourselves.

If old papyri dumped at Oxyrhynchus
　　Survive for centuries in desert sands,
I wonder if posterity will think us
　　A little casual with its demands,
　　When leaving programmes no one understands.
Humanity will face enormous risks
Unless we learn to sand proof all hard disks.

But is there still a future to be had?
　　What are we playing at when architects
Construct for thirty years, no more? If clad
　　In steel or aluminium that reflects
　　The light, it is light and it disconnects
Us from tradition and its stewardship.
Our preference is for present ownership.

The middle classes purchase second homes
　　The length of France and Spain or the Algarve,
No limits how far aspiration roams:
　　The trend is foreign property and carve
　　A backyard there, no matter how you starve
For lack of local knowledge or the language…
As long as you enjoy the *jamon* sandwich…

You lived on different continents when you
　　Were shuttling from New York to Ischia,
But in the '50s that was swell to do,
　　And then the consequence no riskier
　　Than letting to a lover who was friskier
Than any bar fly. Still, you seemed to thrive
There with San Carlo and the opera live.

Forgive me, if we know your private life
    A little better than that noble lord
Byronic: but the man you took for wife,
    Companion, lover (roles that left him bored)
    Showed up a hard fact: if you pick a bawd,
It really is tough love. You did propose
To women, *mais ce n'est pas la même chose.*

And did you know the difference, Wystan, really?
    I guess you did. The record says you did.
I doubt there was a woman loved you clearly,
    Though you were quite domestic. No, I kid
    You not, you liked a household at your bid
And call. You liked your food upon a plate,
But God forbid if anything was late…

Where was I? Ah yes, multiple possession.
    Banks hand out credit like there's no tomorrow,
No matter if a national congression
    Is weak or threatening to beg or borrow.
    Banks know that they can minimize the sorrow:
No matter where it is a family roams,
Collateral remains with native homes.

And when this passion hangs on cheap airfares
    That threaten to increase with every day,
I wonder at the wisdom of time-shares
    Or second homes. How long can people stay
    There when they have them? With the bills to pay
It ends up as a business, what's the betting?
And this is taken mostly by sub-letting.

It's difficult for me to comprehend,
    Perhaps, who currently have two rooms to share
With anyone. Good job I like to spend
    My time here writing. Therefore all is fair
    And square by me. But why must we repair
Abroad? Unless you are a gastronome,
There is good reason we should stay at home.

Yes, global warming.  If the Arctic's melting
    (It always has been, slowly, round the edges),
Antarctica as well takes quite a belting
    From new emissions, so instead of sledges
    And barren coastlines where a penguin fledges,
There may be cool marinas and airports
Where Virgin has some options for resorts.

And then we have our rainforests in the tropics
    Or rather *had* – for we are clearing those
And adding to environmental topics
    Yet one more set of figures that disclose
    How quickly to the mud from which we rose
We will return, especially if we clip
Back Amazonia to a landing strip.

What can we do then, Wystan, to escape
    This desecration of the world? O help
Us learn to keep environments in shape,
    Preserve the coral atoll, rare sea kelp,
    The whale, the seal, and even helpless whelp
Of wolf and jackal and Siberian tiger
On highlands, lowlands or the Russian taiga.

When talk is of ecology, it makes
    One pause to think of earth's fragility
And what we do to raise its seas and lakes,
    But still we have the possibility
    To combat change with some facility:
We could – should this become a water planet –
Grow fins and dive as skilfully as a gannet.

You laugh? We have genetic engineering
    And clever men and women urge the science
Of giving DNA a little steering,
    Creating – as they see it  – an alliance
    With Nature they could turn us into giants,
Mammalian and swimming with no legs,
For all they have to do is doctor eggs.

Ten years ago the Scots cloned our first sheep
   – As if the Cheviots weren't full enough
Already by the natural means to keep
   Us clothed in wool – but, later, was it tough
   For Dolly the Sheep as, prematurely duff
At half her natural span, she had to go
And find whatever maker made her so?

The means is simple: take a nucleus
   And then transfer it, stem cells understand
The rest. But how embarrassing for us
   If we created humans underhand
   Who after half a lifetime had to stand
Before their Maker saying they would rather
Have opted for a more Almighty Father.

It makes you wonder. Would they have a soul
   These creatures, be they he or she? A birth
Miraculous perhaps, but nothing whole
   (Or holy even), with the poor things worth
   But half of us in years. Though if it's girth
You want, geneticists can take a rest,
Obesity will float us with the best.

With global warming giving us more water
   Already adaptation is in place
Among those doing what they didn't oughta
   Till you can barely tell they have a face.
   For looking like a whale there is a case
To live the lifestyle of a couch potato
(It doesn't need an argument from Plato).

And yet biologists have much to do
   Maintaining facts on human evolution.
There's still dissension in the Human Zoo:
   Creationism's counter-revolution
   Regards Darwinian theory a pollution
Of what is fundamentally divine.
It's true the missing link has left no sign,

But if there is no record in the strata
    This hardly can be called as evidence,
Any attempt to look there's a non-starter:
    Without a record, where's the common sense?
    And as to premises, there's no defence
In putting matters geological
Before what's strictly theological.

If God should pose some problems for the laity,
    It's nothing short of what we should expect;
It surely comes as privilege of the Deity
    To keep some answers from our intellect
    No matter how we struggle to detect
Them. But a 3-D model of Dark Matter
Has been mapped out as Hubble gives the 'data'.

Oh, Wystan, could I shine a bit more light
    Here for you! Let's just say it's heavy stuff,
Impossible to see by naked sight
    And even if the calculation's rough
    It seems to be the case that there's enough
Inside the universe's space-time cavity
To make us take it with some gravity.

And as for sub-atomic particles
    The situation similarly is crowded,
New quarks and leptons and such articles
    As gluons, weakons and the like, come shrouded
    In mystery and mysterious names. How did
They think of 'up', 'down', 'strange', 'charmed', 'top' and 'bottom'
When there's no evidence we've really got 'em?

So there you have it, scientific theory
    Has come no closer to the final key
To everything: but still we have to query
    For we will not be satisfied if we
    Cannot unlock the truth of what we see
Out there. But experts in the field of study
All still agree the ground is rather muddy.

I think it's time to take another break.
    As for the science, if you detect a blunder
Then my apologies. I tried to make
    An effort, but then science is a wonder,
    A marvel even. Poets do go under,
Heads spinning with the snippets that we seize
Among its manifold realities...

The snow's still here, it's very late this year,
    The snowdrops aptly named, but – bashful – hide
Beneath the snow crust. Bulbs' green shoots appear,
    The blossom one month early. Such a tide
    Of Nature jumbled. Will it override
Us? On the shed, an icicle makes drops
And in the holly there, a robin hops.

# PART III

And so the secrets of the universe,
    Be they of deep space or molecular
Remain mysterious as (at least in verse)
    The Flying Tricksters of Malekula,
    Those mystic shamans of the secular
Who influenced your 'Airman' (and you) in
*The Orators*.  But now should we begin

A second look at our society?
    There's little distance that we need to go,
If sadly we must leave the piety
    To science behind (the little that I know),
    And after that we will attempt to show
(A little roll upon the kettledrum)
What arts are left in this Millennium.

For binary opposition, we have Centre/
    Margins, not Marx's Superstructure/Base.
Yeats said 'the centre cannot hold', so enter
    Margins wherever they can find a place;
    And from peripheries they garner space
To set up camp, but find things much the same
Now camping up is everybody's game.

The marginal's no longer on the edge,
    You see, nor held in any way 'perverted',
The mere suggestion would be sacrilege
    Today, when everyone has been converted
    And social hierarchy is subverted:
The equal playing field insisting that
Society today is rather flat…

Or squashed and out of shape. You see, if driven
    By motives of equality, no way
Is anything traditional a given:
    We think creatively and who can say
    The next Prime Minister may not be gay?
And where a joint once led to the abyss,
It now helps if you *have* smoked cannabis…

A long, long time ago, of course, the friends
　　Who introduced you to it now behind
You as backbenchers. If you make amends,
　　Apologize for youthful folly, blind
　　As you once were to pleasure, of a mind
To try things – after all, you were a boy –
The public probably will buy the ploy.

If nowadays you find that your MP
　　Comes in a civil partnership – that's same-
Sex marriage to the likes of you or me –
　　It seems the rule each party keeps the name
　　With which they're christened, which is such a shame:
How quaint to find a Mr *and* a Mrs
In those two gentlemen seen blowing kisses.

Of course, the general public must be told
　　Of these developments and they can read
Them in the headlines or a centrefold;
　　It fosters confidence when we concede
　　That newspapers have told the truth: indeed,
Could there be any shadow of a doubt
The trouble that it takes to tweak it out?

The Fourth Estate now Public Inquisition,
　　Its anchormen and women hunt for truth,
Examining political decision
　　With manners that can border on uncouth:
　　Gone are the old days when gin and vermouth
Shared underneath the corridors of power
Confirmed what news went out and at what hour.

Gone, too, are toleration and respect,
　　Along with days of giving up your seat:
It's honourable to stick with the elect,
　　No matter what dirt's sticking to your feet.
　　What would make you resign from the elite?
No, the electorate is stuck with you
Whatever mud is thrown in interview.

For me there's something rather sinister
    About a nation called a 'Nanny State',
Where everything devolves upon a minister
    Who takes it as his job to legislate,
    When local agencies administrate
Far better should they be allowed a hand.
But Whitehall's very slow to understand.

We keep a close watch on communities
    By distant means: the cameras of Big Brother
Can capture many opportunities
    That people use to make a spot of bother:
    If we could delegate to one another
The task, O what a world that it would be
Without surveillance from CCTV!

There is a shortage of intelligence
    At work: the footage shot in shopping mall
Acquires importance and an influence
    At other levels. Now it has us all
    Concerned with our appearances – no small
Coincidence. No matter where you go
We seem to be obsessed with outward show.

This, with our mania for celebrity,
    Has taken up the world's attention, so
To make a comment with integrity
    Is now impossible, the media go
    Invariably to who stars in the show,
The only interest is the marketplace
And selling an already well-known face.

What was exotic or Bohemian,
    Or outraged English *sang froid* with a smile,
Even the lowest academian
    Can see has been converted into 'style';
    There is no content now – not by a mile –
Just as there's 'chocolate' and there's 'chocolate flavour',
And passé rock stars passing as a raver.

Perhaps we do need anthropology
    To understand the tribal pull within
A culture that – without apology –
    Can shamelessly appropriate and spin
    A fashionable deception out to win
A prize? Is there no strength to stand alone
Instead of standing as an ersatz clone?

I recall last year's Eurovision Song
    Contest (now don't pretend you didn't watch
It in Kirchstetten – *though* I may be wrong):
    Once yodelling maidens, bouffant hair, top notch
    Presenters in tuxedos, now they scotch
The competition decked as Finnish trolls
And horror rock comes top in mainstream polls.

So nothing's sacred, everything is plundered,
    No boundary is seen as sacrosanct.
When 'Jesus Jeans' was launched, the media thundered,
    But then again Madonna should be thanked
    For giving them a name that could be banked –
I'm sorry, *ranked* – up there among the stars
That glitter in the heavenly clubs and bars.

You missed out on the Puritan, escaped
    It would be truer to say and wisely so:
You never would have wished to be red-taped
    And in a court case have to undergo
    A grilling from a homophobic so-
And-so, then follow down the weary trail
That carried Oscar Wilde to Reading Gaol.

Today men take a secondary role
    As reparation for the sins gone by
That kept a woman's life from being whole,
    Accepting they must work now, with a sigh
    That he's at home, redundant; so both try,
Him holding down the home for her career
And she out with her colleagues for a beer.

And if she's late back home, it doesn't matter,
　　All meals are handled in the microwave,
There's everything from rice to seafood platter,
　　The TV upstairs has the kids behave
　　Before they sneak off to another rave,
While he thinks of retraining driving trucks
Or at a Borders check out selling books.

For what? So that his daughters can go out
　　In stylish mode? A simulated night's
Celebrity to magnify a bout
　　Of birthday binging may cut down on fights,
　　But as a fashion, well, it stands to rights
That, like the Lottery, it's one more tax
Upon the less well off that we should axe.

Amazingly these hen nights for the girls
　　Extend to hiring stretch white limousines
And copying the get-ups and kiss curls
　　From *glamour* not from *fashion* magazines,
　　Where youthful wannabees still in their teens
Compete in how much they can drop a stitch
As if the paparazzi staked the pitch.

I make no judgement here, only report
　　An interest in cultural levelling
Where rich from poor is difficult to sort
　　Out in the fashionable dishevelling.
　　It seems to be the less you wear's the thing
And no respect for clothing any more
Means everything hangs out from rich to poor.

And in the face of cultural collapse
　　Female celebs try hard by dressing down
In jeans and little knitted woollen caps,
　　Or draped in something like a dressing gown
　　(A wrap dress, is it?) when they go to town,
Unshaven men in T-shirts, shades and boots
Beside them sporting highlights to the roots.

It helps street credibility to sin
    A little with your syntax and your grammar.
'Well, rocket science, it ain't'… you blink and grin.
    The speaker, who is not from Alabama,
    Is happily permitted this to hammer
Home a point. If correct in speech it ain't,
Well, who aspires to be a language saint?

There have been books about the tongue's survival,
    With warnings that it looks about to sink
To media slang unless there be revival
    Of teaching grammar's rules and pen and ink
    (Not sure where they come in, but it's a link),
And punctuation always caused a fuss
Until it came supported by Lynne Truss.

But if we turn towards the use of words
    In general or particular, well you,
Wystan, could ably round them up in herds,
    (Perhaps in isolated ranches, too,
    In later years) a veritable zoo,
When you were darling of the media,
Your diction an encyclopaedia!

But humour is the best didactic means
    Despite the dreadful risk of seeming light.
Today you see professors wearing jeans
    Pontificating on the box with some delight
    In trendy language and against the sight
Of landscapes with the best historic views,
Like Simon Schama or Bethany Hughes.

I could go on. How we communicate
    Is still a mystery, the great divide
Of common language keeps us separate.
    No matter what the cause identified,
    Let fruitful ambiguity provide
Us with its everlasting crossword clues,
For who would gag the language of the Muse?

Or clip the viewless wings of poetry?
  Remember when it looked like shopping lists,
One word per line in perfect symmetry,
  Composed by members of the latest '–ists'?
  All mercifully gone. But there persists
A L-A-N-G-U-A-G-E school that has its poets cloak
Work in a language no one ever spoke.

You don't recall?  I should exemplify,
  Despite some difficulty with the scheme
Rime royal offers. Hm, now let me try…
  It's yet another aspect of extreme
  Art, stream of consciousness, perhaps a dream…
**SPACE** (here I think you fill in all the rest)
**Is/LIFE=d EAT h/ US inside a BUS stop/West**

You see? Apart from spacing out the words,
  It uses subtle interplay of case,
Where deconstructing hierarchy girds
  With meaning; but with meaning out of place,
  And words unstable as an interface
Then defamiliarisation is *de trop*,
I'd say. And obvious? Well, *there* you go…

A decade later and a special curse
  Came haunting in 'New Formalism'. 'New'
Was pushing it for what was really verse
  That's always been around, if kept from view
  By editors who thought it *ingénu*
(The types who think that you're not trying hard
Unless you sign up to the avant-garde).

In prose we have the novelist who's seen
  Life in the raw and thinks you will be smitten
By hearing how we combat the Machine
  And have to bite our nails and be hard bitten.
  The only query being: is it well written?
The way they pound the flesh until it's red
Suggests some things are better left unsaid.

We still have family sagas and the loss
    Of innocence in fanciful *memoires*;
With truth content as slender as Kate Moss
    They have become my ultimate *bête noir*
    So full of fiction and invention are
They, detailing each savage cut and blow,
One wonders how the truth could ever show.

I don't think you were keen on film or dance
    Or even plays beyond the ones you wrote
(But might have loved to see Nijinsky prance
    About). On music I must add a note,
    In case the strains you hear are too remote.
If there is one thing that I'm sure inspires
It would be coming from the Baltic choirs.

And serious music? Orchestrated noise,
    That's all. Contemporary plunk and dot
Composed by overeducated boys
    For anything from harp to coffeepot
    Is like a soundtrack searching for the plot,
A ghost of nineteenth century programmatic
Lost in atonal traces, achromatic.

You seemed to like a painting and admired
    Old Masters in the Musée des Beaux Arts.
But painting is so flat and artists tired
    Of it and adding to the senses far
    More fun to execute: art's on a par
With all that we experience around
Us: lights and noise in ambient surround!

There's such a forceful flow in every stream
    I really wonder where to make a start…
The fashion tends, as ever, to extreme
    Obsessions banged up in the name of art.
    When Andy Warhol jumped up on the cart
And printed an electric chair in silk
Screen, his disciples had a theme to milk.

So, death in pastel colours or in plastic,
    Set in formaldehyde or camera shot
For installation has to be fantastic.
    Entrepreneurial artists hit the spot
    And spite our pleasures, railing we are not
Immortal. Seems to me the same old story
The Middle Ages called *memento mori*.

Art should be dangerous and undermine
    Outmoded preconceptions, turn the tide
And make us connoisseurs, not Philistine,
    And show the long experimental slide
    Turns out to be entirely justified;
Although what recently was in the Tate
Was dangerous enough to contemplate.

Postmodernism's only referential,
    With no originality at work,
As long as it avoids the reverential
    When lifting someone else's stylish quirk:
    Take only what will raise a little smirk,
And gesture to the images gone by,
Recycle with a twist, then kiss goodbye!

It is a form of New Scholasticism
    That dominates the visual arts today.
No wonder that it's forced on us a schism.
    If artists call it art, then who dare say
    It's not? So Marcel Duchamp still holds sway,
A final desperate finger of regard
Floats on the last waves of the avant-garde.

The graft is done by experts in a trade
    Who fashion what the good artists require
In porcelain, cement or even jade;
    Except that first sketch or moquette in wire
    Will gain whatever price artists desire:
Conceptual art trips lightly and ethereal,
But when it comes to payment, that's material.

Oh, yes, it is a rollercoaster ride
    And you can take all with you as you go
From strength to strength, eventually inside
    10 Downing Street, where you can get to know
    More exhibitionists than you could throw
A paintbrush at... *A paintbrush? Oh, what's that?*
*There may be one left at my Camden flat,*

*Stuck in a vase upon a window ledge*
    *Where someone dubbed it 'Art's Conceptual Flower'!*
*Yes, all those bristles looking like a hedge...*
    *Perhaps I'll paint them green to show the power*
    *Of natural hog hair bristling in a shower*
*Of sunlight, representing... No, I doubt*
*It, man, with representation still so **out**...*

But games of 'risk' come coupled with 'disaster'.
    A work that's frozen in reality
Can come unstuck and there's no sticking plaster
    Can ever bind it up, for what you see
    Is water everywhere or blood or tea,
Depending on whatever's been infused,
And even body solids may be used.

And if that sort of work creates bad odour,
    Then you can simply use your body, thus
Create a synthesis – perhaps a coda –
    That finally fuses art and life: no fuss,
    No sweat, you are a walking omnibus
Of art, it oozes out of every pore
(If I may multiply the metaphor).

We take the modern artists at their word,
    A work of art is what they say it is.
Perhaps it looks uncannily absurd,
    Perhaps it is a striptease or a quiz
    Or patches on a bathrobe, hers and his:
You must keep silent and believe it so,
And never mention Michelangelo.

The thing is Buonarrotti worked in stone.
    It's not an easy thing to work in hard
Materials and difficult to hone;
    But in the end the marble in his yard
    Was fashioned into works we still regard
With interest, even if his taste in men
Is something that would make you think again

(And that says nothing of his women). But
    You catch my drift here: your material
Will make the business worth it in the cut.
    I have no wish to be funereal,
    It's not as if I missed my breakfast cereal,
But there's no wonder if its sales move fast,
Contemporary art was never made to last.

In art, exaggeration rules the day,
    The thing is how you do it. If you think
Eternal monuments have feet of clay
    That seems to summarize us; if you shrink
    From tests of being memorable or blink
At any heartfelt feelings left inside,
It serves no purpose saying that we tried.

So what will we bequeath to seas and shores
    The remnants of the land after tsunamis,
Earthquakes and headaches and the lonely spores
    Left to inhabit Earth after the armies
    Of mass destruction showed us where the harm is?
A desperate failure to appreciate
That summer's lease has all too short a date.

The weather's blowing hot and cold, a bit
    Like me perhaps and as I see wind shake
New daffodils and marvel how they sit
    It out, so like the robin on its rake
    Perched on the edge of things, but with a stake
So deep in them that nature will survive
Perhaps no matter what we may contrive.

Here it's still spring and now the March winds blow
    Down from the North with storm clouds full of hail
And on the uplands even falls of snow
    Predicted. So I sit here in a gale
    And watch the branches bending in the vale,
Black whips tormented in a livid sky.
And *ut pictura* poetry? Well, I try.

*

# PART IV

So time runs out and urges me to close,
    Not having taken too much of it up,
I trust. And as for other readers, those
    Brave two or three prepared to take the cup,
    The saucer and the biscuit – even sup –
My heartfelt thanks; and also to the stanza
For kindly housing this extravaganza.

I left you in a travesty of March
    And who knows what will really come this spring...
I dare say we will recognize the larch
    And other leafy denizens that bring
    Relief to skylines, sheltering birds that sing...
Oh drat, Romantics made you turn neuralgic,
But then they sometimes make me feel nostalgic...

When all you had to do to be a poet
    Was charge about the English countryside,
Inspired if you could gather seed then sow it
    Or hook a country maiden for a bride.
    Then ten young children whom you must provide
For? Come to think of it, the Modern Age
Is better than it looks upon the page.

But what of me? Oh, Wystan, I'd be flattered
    Only to think you really meant to ask.
It's not as if a poet ever mattered
    (Well, not like you), but it's a simple task.
    And so with your *nil obstat* let me bask
A moment in historical reflection,
That is, if I have any recollection.

My grandfathers did well in cotton, lost
    The lot and therefore made no great impression
Upon the nation's wealth. It was the cost
    Of living through what was the Great Depression,
    Which passed you by, as you had a profession.
My parents were, like yours, at best ill matched.
The house we lived in small, semi-detached.

A prototype of comprehensive school
    Fostered the basic skills, if nothing more
Than how to stop a nose bleed, break a rule
    Or two – or even hide out in a store
    Room during trig; the rest was Elsinore,
Revenge and tragedy were engineered
Among the A stream; but the E was feared.

If put on track as an economist,
    Geology meant I could take a trip
To Iceland, thus I braved the Northern mist,
    Volcanic deserts, braided rivers, drip
    Of rain, and took along for fellowship
Your 'Letter to Lord Byron'. As a guide
To glaciers its success was qualified.

My other book was *Crime and Punishment*,
    A strange choice at the age of seventeen,
But very good for reading in a tent
    Or in a cabin if the sea's serene;
    Not that there was much time to read between
Rock breaking and the field geology
Siberian in its topology.

Too commonsensical or passionate,
    I passed up on a university
The first time round and, as a drop-out, ate
    The bitter fruit of my perversity;
    (Not understanding its diversity)
Was postman, dustman, man that cut the grass,
And ended up in Italy, second class;

Then, courtesy of R. and E. B. Browning,
    Inhabited the flat at Casa Guidi
During the years when Italy was drowning
    In violence, terrorism and quite needy
    Of some stability; if it was seedy,
As a writer I enjoyed my first success
With several pieces for the *TLS*.

And then to Oxford, where I had my fill
    Of scholarship, a doctorate too late
To cash in on, and so – MA, D. Phil –
    What could I do but, like you, educate?
    And how the modern theorists loved to hate
A medievalist – me for a start –
Despite my reading Derrida and Barthes!

Eventually, of course, I left the rush.
    A college lecturer with no tenure fails
To keep a grip on things, lost in the push
    For honours, publications, but the scales
    May tip back in my favour. It entails
Good fortune and the patronage of friends.
Of course, a letter may bring dividends.

So back in my Bohemia, I write this:
    An open letter asking for no cash,
Perhaps a little credit up in bliss,
    That's all. No matter if a cheque should flash
    Before my eyes in payment as I dash
This off, it comes to you wrapped in rime royal,
With you for glitter and me as the foil.

But then, like me, you were the Suffering Man,
    Although for you a Suffering Sphinx would be
More apt. How much you would have loved to swan
    About the salons, perfect at a tea,
    Pontificating to it beautifully
On love, although – no Housman – you had more
A taste that's fraught with violence and the poor.

(Oh, by the way, a footnote for you, –  now
    I know it's way beyond its sell by date –
But this is not the breaking news or Dow
    Jones daily average, but yet of late
    As poet of love you met a better fate
On film and though it is unusual
Starred in *Four Weddings and a Funeral*.)

A democratic leveller in verse,
    Perhaps postmodernist before its time
You deftly mingled ballad metres, terse
    Reflections, highbrow terms and bawdy rhyme
    With registers that turned round on a dime.
And here the blame cannot be television,
More your antipathy to vatic vision.

You could not stand the Lakeland Poets or Keats,
    Although we know you had a softer spot
For Byron – whether this was for his feats
    Of versifying could be true or not –
    But possibly his vices made you hot.
No doubt for doing what was not allowed
He left the country underneath a cloud.

Perhaps you felt some sympathy with this?
    And whether led by innocence or guile –
Or was the Promised Land just promised bliss? –
    But in America you lived in style,
    The loft flat of a Greenwich Village pile.
I guess you hoped that here you could begin
Again in language turning mandarin.

But we admire the bulk of what you wrote,
    In love or out, upon these Saxon shores;
The rest becomes a little more remote:
    I find 'In Praise of Limestone' rather bores
    Me… What about the *mezzogiorno* whores?
If cheap, at least, they could be colourful,
While limestone at its best is very dull.

In your day it was fine to mention 'pylon',
    Indeed, it came to be thought *de rigeur*,
Although there was a sticking point with 'nylon',
    Which all of you regarded with hauteur,
    Perhaps it seemed to be less him more *her*…
We had to wait for Skylon and the New
Elizabethan Age when Larkin's crew

Could wallow *en abîme* in the demotic,
 When swearing generally came to be allowed,
As long as it was purely anecdotic –
 Something that you would hear among a crowd
 Of chaps, perhaps. At first, you know, it wowed
Us silly; now we've wallowed in the muck,
We exercise a little nip and tuck.

Love gave no inspiration – it is said –
 Or no distinctive rapture made you odd
Like some of those Romantics, but the head
 Too firmly ruled the heart and made you plod,
 A puritan whose hard work ethic God
Would have approved. Now in your other world,
I hope you sit ecstatic, wings unfurled.

Your poetry of prayer and vision, hope
 In something better for humanity,
And pedagogic patience had us cope
 And helped us all retain our sanity
 Despite the world, its chaos and its vanity.
So let us chorus with a rousing voice
And toast the poet who taught us to rejoice!

If you would pray for us while strumming hymns
 Upon your old celestial Joanna,
Pausing to sip ambrosial-style Pimm's
 After one's best camp Noel Coward manner,
 We should be grateful, gladly raise the banner
Again for you another hundred years
From now. But in the meantime, Wystan, cheers!

*Woodstock, January - April 2007*

# Notes

Part of this poem was first published in *Agenda*, vol. 43, nos 2-3 Spring 2008, pp. 23-31 under the title 'To W. H. Auden in Heaven: A Letter in his Centenary Year'.

p 9  Jeff Nuttall (1933-2004) painter, poet and author of *Bomb Culture* (1968).

p 10  Edward Mendelson, editor of *The English Auden* (1977).

p 13  'why the Japanese/Invaded her in 1938'. See W. H. Auden and Christopher Isherwood, *Journey to a War* (1939).

p 13  'low dishonest decade', see Auden's 'September 1, 1939'.

p 14  ibid: 'What all schoolchildren learn, / Those to whom evil is done / Do evil in return.'

p 21  'in nylon cubes', see Auden's 'Metalogue to *The Magic Flute*'.

p 22  'Fahrenheit 451'. The temperature at which paper ignites.  See Ray Bradbury, *Fahrenheit 451* (1953), a novel set a future dystopia where books are banned and burned.

p 23  'Oxyrhynchus'. Archaeological site in Upper Egypt yielding a wealth of papyri.

p 23  The Real Teatro San Carlo in Naples is the world's oldest continuously active opera house.

p 24  'the man you took for wife'. Chester Kallman (1921-1975), poet, librettist and translator.

p 34  The 51st Eurovision Song Contest (2006) was won by Lordi, the Finnish 'horror rock' band.

p 36  See Lynne Truss, *Eats, Shoots & Leaves* (2003).

p 39  'what recently was in the Tate'. In October, 2006, German artist Carsten Höller exhibited five giant playground slides under the title '*Test Site*' in Tate Modern's Turbine Hall.

p 47  See Auden's sonnet 'A. E. Housman', 'Food was his public love, his private lust / Something to do with violence and the poor.'